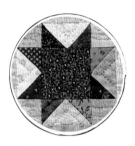

BLACKBERG EDITION

11 Beloved Quilts That Stand the Test of Time

Cindy Blackberg

Blackberg Edition: 11 Beloved Quilts That Stand
the Test of Time
© 2021 by Cindy Blackberg

Martingale®
18939 120th Ave. NE, Ste. 101
Bothell, WA 98011-9511 USA
ShopMartingale.com

Printed in Hong Kong
26 25 24 23 22 21   8 7 6 5 4 3 2 1

Library of Congress Cataloging-in-Publication Data is
available upon request.

ISBN: 978-1-68356-113-2

MISSION STATEMENT

We empower makers who use fabric and yarn
to make life more enjoyable.

CREDITS

**PUBLISHER AND
CHIEF VISIONARY OFFICER**
Jennifer Erbe Keltner

CONTENT DIRECTOR
Karen Costello Soltys

DESIGN MANAGER
Adrienne Smitke

MANAGING EDITOR
Tina Cook

PRODUCTION MANAGER
Regina Girard

**ACQUISITIONS AND
DEVELOPMENT EDITOR**
Laurie Baker

**COVER AND
BOOK DESIGNER**
Mia Mar

COPY EDITOR
Jen Hornsby

LOCATION PHOTOGRAPHER
Adam Albright

STUDIO PHOTOGRAPHER
Brent Kane

ILLUSTRATOR
Sandy Loi

SPECIAL THANKS
*Photography for this book was taken at the homes of:
Tracie Fish in Kenmore, Washington,
Julie Smiley in Des Moines, Iowa, and
Libby Warnken in Ankeny, Iowa.*

CONTENTS

INTRODUCTION

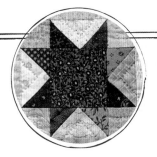

BRINGING THE PAST INTO THE PRESENT is something that I enjoy doing as a quilter. Knowing that I'm creating quilts using the same block patterns as my quilting foremothers and replicating them in fabrics that resemble the prints and colors they used gives me a connection to a time when patchwork quilts were a part of everyday life.

I am especially fond of scrap quilts from the late 1800s. Unlike many of those makers, I didn't learn to quilt when I was girl. However, I'd always sewed, making my own clothes while growing up. The desire to quilt came in 1974 when my two sons were young and I wanted to make quilts for them. Fortunately for me, the nation's bicentennial brought a resurgence of quilting and it wasn't long before I was taking what I had learned and teaching others.

The projects in this book are a compilation of designs that I've created through the years. They're all based on traditional American patchwork blocks, most of them are scrappy, and the majority of them are hand pieced and hand quilted. Handwork is my preference, but I understand that not everyone is like me, so all of the instructions reflect machine piecing. There are two exceptions: Apple of My Eye (page 69) and Little Houses (page 73) are both much better suited to hand piecing, so the instructions are written to reflect that.

Because I love to do handwork, I've included basic information for how to hand piece on page 78. Each project also includes the patterns to make templates for hand piecing the blocks should you want to go that route. Personally, I think it's very relaxing, and I find it's often even quicker than machine piecing. I hope you'll give it a try!

No matter which piecing method you choose to embrace, I hope you'll find time to bring a piece of the past into the present to be enjoyed for future generations to come.

Cindy

CHARMING CHURN DASH

Finished quilt size: 31½" × 31½"   Finished block size: 3" × 3"

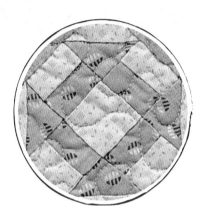

Everyday items often provide the inspiration for quilt blocks. Originating around the early to mid-1800s, the Churn Dash block was so named because the shape created by the dark outer pieces is similar to the shape of a butter churn, while the center square resembles the stick or dash.

Materials

Yardage is based on 42"-wide fabric.

5" × 5" square *each* of 25 assorted dark prints for blocks

5" × 5" square *each* of 25 assorted light prints for blocks

⅞ yard of light blue stripe for sashing and border

¼ yard of red print for sashing squares and border corners

¼ yard of brown check for setting triangles

¼ yard of blue-and-brown plaid for single-fold binding

1 yard of fabric for backing

36" × 36" square of batting

Cutting

Measurements are for machine piecing and include ¼"-wide seam allowances. If you prefer to hand piece the blocks, refer to "For Hand Piecers" on page 11 and do not cut the pieces in this list that are marked with an asterisk.

From *each* dark square, cut:

2 squares, 1⅞" × 1⅞"; cut in half diagonally to make 4 triangles*

4 rectangles, 1" × 1½"*

From *each* light square, cut:

2 squares, 1⅞" × 1⅞"; cut in half diagonally to make 4 triangles*

4 rectangles, 1" × 1½"*

1 square, 1½" × 1½"*

From the *lengthwise grain* of the light blue stripe, cut:

4 strips, 3¼" × 26"

64 rectangles, 2" × 3½"

Continued on page 9

Designed and pieced by Cindy Blackberg; machine quilted by Cathy Witt

Continued from page 7

From the red print, cut:

2 strips, 2" × 42"; crosscut into 40 squares, 2" × 2"

4 squares, 3¼" × 3¼"

From the brown check, cut:

4 squares, 5½" × 5½"; cut into quarters diagonally
to make 16 triangles

From the blue-and-brown plaid, cut:

Enough 1¼"-wide *bias* strips to equal 136" when
pieced together end to end *OR* 4 straight-grain
strips, 1¼" × 42"

Making the Blocks

Sew all pieces with right sides together, using a
¼" seam allowance. Press the seam allowances
as indicated by the arrows.

1. Select the pieces cut from one light 5" square
and one dark 5" square.

2. Join a light and a dark triangle along the long
diagonal edges. Press. Repeat to make a total of
four corner units. Each unit should measure 1½"
square, including seam allowances.

Make 4 corner units,
1½" × 1½".

3. Sew a light rectangle to a dark rectangle along
the long edges to make a side unit. Press. Repeat
to make a total of four side units measuring 1½"
square, including seam allowances.

Make 4 side units,
1½" × 1½".

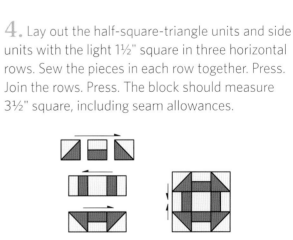

4. Lay out the half-square-triangle units and side
units with the light 1½" square in three horizontal
rows. Sew the pieces in each row together. Press.
Join the rows. Press. The block should measure
3½" square, including seam allowances.

Churn Dash block,
3½" × 3½"

5. Repeat steps 1–4 to make a total of 25 blocks.

Assembling the Quilt Top

1. Refer to the quilt assembly diagram below to arrange the blocks, the blue stripe 2" × 3½" sashing rectangles, the red 2" sashing squares, and the brown check setting triangles in diagonal rows. Sew together the pieces in each row. Press. Join the rows. Add the corner triangles last. Press.

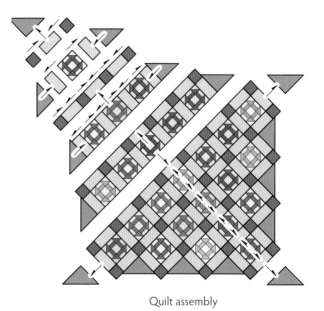

Quilt assembly

2. Press the top and trim the edges ¼" from the points of the sashing rectangles. The quilt top should measure 26" square, including seam allowances.

Trim ¼" from point.

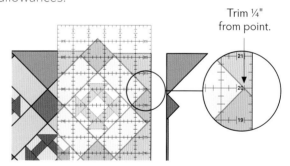

3. Sew blue stripe 3¼" × 26" strips to opposite sides of the quilt top. Press. Sew the red 3¼" squares to each end of the remaining two blue stripe 3¼" × 26" strips. Press. Join these strips to the top and bottom of the quilt top.

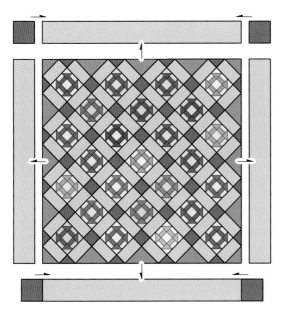

Adding the border

Finishing

For more details on any of the following steps, visit ShopMartingale.com/HowtoQuilt for free downloadable information.

1. Layer the quilt top, batting, and backing. Baste the layers together.

2. Quilt by hand or machine. The quilt shown is machine quilted with an allover stippling design.

3. Use the plaid 1¼"-wide strips to make the single-fold binding, and then attach the binding to the quilt. Enjoy!

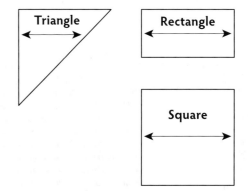

LITTLE LEMOYNE STARS

Finished quilt size: 20¾" × 25"   Finished block size: 3" × 3"

It's futile to resist the allure of these charming little blocks. Even though they have set-in seams, like anything worth doing, a little practice will have you wondering what all the fuss is about.

Materials

Yardage is based on 42"-wide fabric.

1⅛" × 25" strip *each* of 12 assorted dark prints for blocks

¼ yard of light print for blocks

⅓ yard of blue print for setting triangles

⅝ yard of light double border print (a print with a border on *both* selvage edges) or print with a repeating pattern for sashing*

⅜ yard of brown check for border

¼ yard of blue-and-brown stripe for single-fold binding

¾ yard of fabric for backing

25" × 29" piece of batting

*Select a print with a pattern from which you can cut identical 2¼"-wide strips. The print shown uses a repeating pattern that runs in stripes parallel to the selvage.

Cutting

Measurements are for machine piecing and include ¼"-wide seam allowances. If you prefer to hand piece the blocks, refer to "For Hand Piecers" on page 20 and do not cut the pieces in this list that are marked with an asterisk.

From the light print, cut:

1 strip, 2½" × 42"; crosscut into 12 squares, 2½" × 2½". Cut each square into quarters diagonally to make 48 triangles.*

2 strips, 1⅜" × 42"; crosscut into 48 squares, 1⅜" × 1⅜"*

From the blue print, cut:

1 strip, 3" × 42"; crosscut into 6 squares, 3" × 3". Cut each square in half diagonally to make 12 small triangles.

1 strip, 5½" × 42"; crosscut into 5 squares, 5½" × 5½". Cut each square into quarters diagonally to make 20 large triangles (2 are extra).

From the *lengthwise grain* of the border print, cut:

2 identical strips, 2¼" × 17½"

Continued on page 14

Continued from page 13

From the brown check, cut:

4 strips, 2½" × 24"

From the blue-and-brown stripe, cut:

Enough 1¼"-wide *bias* strips to equal 102" when pieced together end to end *OR* 3 straight-grain strips, 1¼" × 42"

Making the Blocks

Sew all pieces with right sides together, using a ¼" seam allowance. Press the seam allowances as indicated by the arrows.

1. For machine piecing, align the 45° line of an acrylic ruler with the bottom of a dark print 1⅛" × 25" strip and trim the left end of the strip as shown. Measuring from the angled cut, make eight more cuts at the same angle, 1⅛" apart, to yield eight diamonds for one block. Repeat with the remaining dark print 1⅛" × 25" strips. For hand piecing, use the diamond template (pattern on page 20) to cut eight diamonds from each dark 1⅛" × 25" strip.

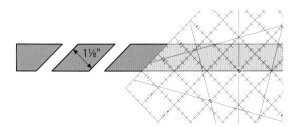

Cut 8 diamonds per strip.

2. Mark the seam intersection with a dot on the wrong side of each dark diamond and each light triangle and square as shown.

3. Using the diamonds cut from one print, place two diamonds right sides together and sew one side as shown. Backstitch at the corners, but avoid stitching into the seam allowances. Repeat to make a total of four pairs.

Make 4 pairs.

4. Join two pairs of diamonds to make a half-star unit, and then sew the two half-star units together to complete the star. Before pressing, undo two stitches in the seam allowance at the center of the star. This will allow the seam allowances to be pressed in a clockwise direction, helping to distribute the bulk at the center of the block. Be careful not to stretch the bias edge of the diamonds as you press.

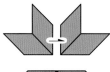 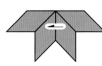 

5. Sew light triangles between the points on all four sides of a star. With right sides together, match the points of a diamond with a triangle. Stitch the seam, clip the threads, and remove the pieces from the machine. Match the other point of the light triangle to the adjacent diamond and sew. Repeat with all four light triangles. Press the seam allowances of the set-in light pieces in a counterclockwise direction.

 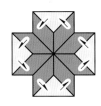

6. Inset a light square into each corner of the star in the same manner to complete the block. Press the seam allowances of the squares in a counterclockwise direction, as described above. The block should measure 3½" square, including seam allowances.

LeMoyne Star block,
3½" × 3½"

7. Repeat steps 3–6 to make a total of 12 blocks.

Designed, pieced, and hand quilted by Cindy Blackberg

Assembling the Quilt Top

1. Lay out four LeMoyne Star blocks, six blue large triangles, and four blue small corner triangles in diagonal rows as shown. Sew the pieces in each row together. Join the rows. Then add the small triangles last. The row should measure 4¾" × 17½", including seam allowances. Repeat to make a total of three rows.

2. Refer to the quilt assembly diagram below to lay out the three block rows and two border print sashing strips in alternating positions. Join the rows and strips. The quilt top should measure 16¾" × 17½", including seam allowances.

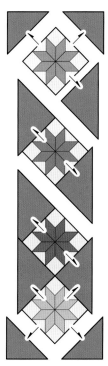

Make 3 rows,
4¾" × 17½".

Quilt assembly

3. Refer to "Making Borders with Mitered Corners" on page 18 to sew the brown check 2¼" × 24" strips to the quilt top and miter the corners. Press the seam allowances toward the border.

Mitered corners add a classic touch to any quilt border, and they're really not difficult to sew. Measure and sew accurately and you'll be a pro in no time.

1. The length of the border strips has already been calculated for the projects in this book, so just cut the strips as instructed and proceed to step 2. If you want to add a mitered border to a quilt top or use mitered corners instead of butted corners, here's the formula. Measure each side of the quilt top and add twice the width of the border strip. Add at least another 2" to this measurement for extra insurance. For example, if your quilt top measures 16¾" × 17½" and your border strips are cut 2¼" wide, you'll need two strips at least 23¼" long and two strips at least 24" long. To simplify the cutting, when strips are close in length, I just cut to the longest length. If your quilt has more than one border, calculate the size of the quilt top after adding each border and cut your strips, using the same formula.

2. Fold the quilt in half and mark the centers of the quilt edges. Fold each border strip in half crosswise and mark the centers. Measure from the center of the quilt top to the edge to determine half the length of the top. Measuring from the center of each strip, mark the halved quilt-top length on each border. If your quilt has more than one border, sew the strips for each side together along the long edges, matching the centers.

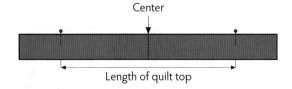

Center

Length of quilt top

3. Working on one side at a time, pin the border strips to the quilt top, matching the centers. Align the marks at each end of the border strip with the ends of the quilt and ease the remainder of the border strip to fit. Stitch the strip to the quilt top, beginning and ending ¼" from the raw edges of the quilt top.

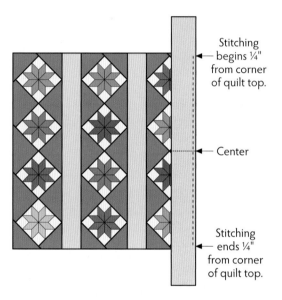

Stitching begins ¼" from corner of quilt top.

Center

Stitching ends ¼" from corner of quilt top.

4. Lay the first corner to be mitered on an ironing board. Fold under one border strip at a 45° angle to the other strip. Press and pin.

5. Fold the quilt in half diagonally, right sides together with the adjacent edges of the border aligned. If necessary, use a ruler and pencil to draw a line on the pressed crease to make the stitching line more visible. Stitch on the pressed crease, sewing from the previous stitching line to the outer edges. If you have multiple borders, be sure to match the seam intersections of each border.

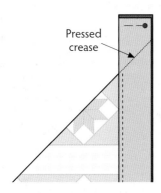

Pressed crease

6. Press the seam allowances open, check the right side of the quilt to make sure the miters are neat with no puckers, and then turn the quilt over and trim away the excess border strips, leaving a ¼" seam allowance.

7. Repeat with the remaining corners.

Finishing

For more details on any of the following steps, visit ShopMartingale.com/HowtoQuilt for free downloadable information.

1. Layer the quilt top, batting, and backing. Baste the layers together.

2. Quilt by hand or machine. The quilt shown is hand quilted with a double row of outline quilting around each block that extends into the border.

3. Use the blue-and-brown stripe 1¼"-wide strips to make the single-fold binding, and then attach the binding to the quilt. Enjoy!

FOR HAND PIECERS

If you find sewing stars on a machine to be tricky where all those seams converge in the center, you may prefer hand piecing because you can put the needle right where you need it. To hand piece the stars, sew the diamonds into pairs and then halves, just as you would for machine piecing, but when you sew the halves together, sew from the outside edge to the center on both halves.

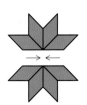

Next, add the background pieces, using what I call the sequential method of sewing. To piece sequentially, start at a corner and work around the star to add each piece. It goes very fast and it's easy!

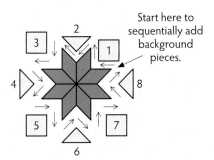

Refer to "Hand-Piecing Basics" on page 78 to make the templates. Use the templates to cut the pieces from the fabrics indicated. Cutting instructions are for the LeMoyne Star blocks only. Patterns do not include seam allowances.

Using the square template, cut:
48 from the light print

Using the diamond template, cut:
48 from the light print

Using the triangle template, cut:
8 from *each* dark strip (96 total)

Optional hand-piecing patterns

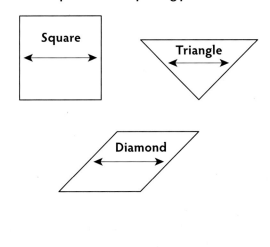

STAR TOSS

Finished quilt size: 40½" × 50½"   Finished block size: 4" × 4"

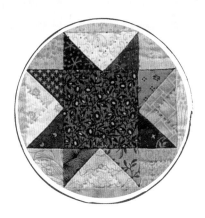

Going to a quilt show is always a blast! In addition to feeling inspired by all the amazing quilts, I can't help bringing home colorful purchases from the fabric vendors. This quilt started with a bundle of dark fat eighths I picked up at a show, and I added scraps of light fabrics from my stash. Star Toss is one of my all-time favorite quilts.

Materials

Yardage is based on 42"-wide fabric.

2⅞ yards *total* of assorted dark prints for blocks, sashing cornerstones, and border

3 yards *total* of assorted medium and light cream and tan prints for blocks, sashing strips, and border (collectively referred to as "lights")

¼ yard of medium tan print for single-fold binding

2⅔ yards of fabric for backing

47" × 57" piece of batting

Cutting

Measurements are for machine piecing and include ¼"-wide seam allowances. If you prefer to hand piece the blocks, refer to "For Hand Piecers" on page 27 and do not cut the pieces in this list that are marked with an asterisk.

From the dark prints, cut a *total* of:

63 squares, 2½" × 2½"*

164 rectangles, 1½" × 2½"*

504 squares, 1½" × 1½", for blocks*

80 squares, 1½" × 1½", for sashing

From the light prints, cut a *total* of:

4 squares, 2½" × 2½"

142 rectangles, 1½" × 4½"

252 rectangles, 1½" × 2½"*

580 squares, 1½" × 1½"

From the medium tan print, cut:

Enough 1¼"-wide *bias* strips to equal 192" when pieced together end to end *OR* 5 straight-grain strips, 1¼" × 42"

Making the Blocks

Sew all pieces with right sides together, using a ¼" seam allowance. Press the seam allowances as indicated by the arrows.

1. Select one dark 2½" square, four light 1½" × 2½" rectangles, eight dark 1½" squares, and four light 1½" squares. Draw a diagonal line from corner to corner on the wrong side of each dark 1½" square.

Achieving Random Scrappiness

Here is where the fun begins! For the perfect fabric mix, just toss the light squares into a bag. Do the same with your light rectangles, large dark squares, and small dark squares, and then pull out what you need for each block as you stitch. It is so much fun to randomly choose what you need each time you make a block.

2. Lay a marked dark square on one end of a light 1½" × 2½" rectangle, right sides together. Stitch on the marked line. Trim ¼" from the stitching line. Press. Repeat on the opposite end of the rectangle to make a flying-geese unit. Press. Repeat to make a total of four flying-geese units measuring 1½" × 2½", including seam allowances.

Make 4 units,
1½" × 2½".

3. Lay out the four flying-geese units and the remaining pieces selected in step 1 in three horizontal rows. Sew the pieces in each row together. Press. Join the rows to complete the Star block. Press. The block should measure 4½" square, including seam allowances.

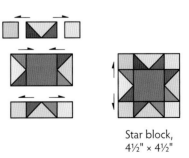

Star block,
4½" × 4½"

4. Repeat steps 1–3 to make a total of 63 blocks.

Designed, pieced, and hand quilted by Cindy Blackberg

Assembling the Quilt Top

1. Refer to the quilt assembly diagram to lay out the blocks, the light 1½" × 4½" sashing rectangles, and the dark 1½" sashing squares in 10 sashing rows and nine block rows as shown. Sew the pieces in each row together. Press. Join the rows. Press. The quilt top should measure 36½" × 46½", including seam allowances.

2. Using the remaining dark 1½" × 2½" rectangles and light 1½" squares, refer to step 2 of "Making the Blocks" on page 23 to make 164 flying-geese units measuring 1½" × 2½", including seam allowances.

Make 164 units,
1½" × 2½".

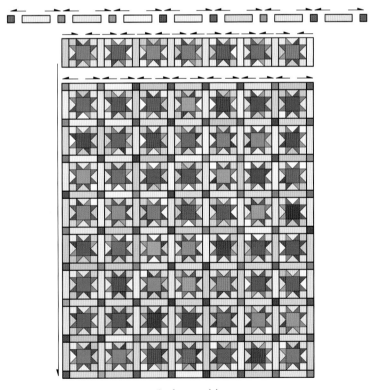

Quilt assembly

3. Referring to the diagram at right, join 46 flying-geese units along their long edges to make a side border measuring 2½" × 46½", including seam allowances. Press. Repeat to make a total of two side borders. Sew the borders to the sides of the quilt top, paying close attention to the direction of the flying-geese units. Press.

Make 2 side borders,
2½" × 46½".

4. In the same manner, join 36 flying-geese units along their long edges. Press. Add a light 2½" square to each end of the strip to make the top border. Press. The border should measure 2½" × 40½", including seam allowances. Repeat to make the bottom border.

Make 2 top/bottom borders,
2½" × 40½".

5. Join the top and bottom borders to the quilt top, again paying close attention to the direction of the flying-geese units. They are flying in a counterclockwise direction around the quilt.

Adding the border

BLACKBERG EDITION

Finishing

For more details on any of the following steps, visit ShopMartingale.com/HowtoQuilt for free downloadable information.

1. Layer the quilt top, batting, and backing. Baste the layers together.

2. Quilt by hand or machine. The quilt shown is outline quilted by hand. An on-point square is quilted in each Star block center.

3. Use the tan 1¼"-wide strips to make single-fold binding, and then attach the binding to the quilt. Enjoy!

FOR HAND PIECERS

Because same-size flying-geese units are used for the blocks and border, rather than making flying-geese units as instructed in steps 1 and 2 of "Making the Blocks," make a flying-geese unit by sewing a small triangle to each diagonal edge of a large triangle. Refer to page 23 for more information.

. . . .

Refer to "Hand-Piecing Basics" on page 78 to make the templates. Use the templates to cut the pieces from the fabrics indicated. Cutting instructions are for the Star blocks and flying-geese border units. Patterns do not include seam allowances.

Using the large square template, cut:
63 from the assorted dark prints

Using the small square template, cut:
252 from the assorted light prints

Using the large triangle template, cut:
252 from the assorted light prints
164 from the assorted dark prints

Using the small triangle template, cut:
504 from the assorted dark prints
328 from the assorted light prints

Optional hand-piecing patterns

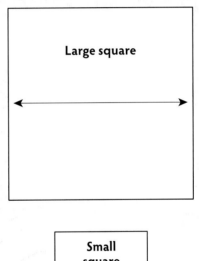

Large square

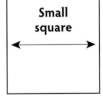

Small square

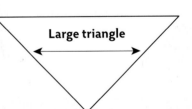

Large triangle

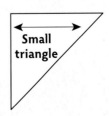

Small triangle

BLUE BASKETS

Finished quilt size: 42" × 42"   Finished block size: 7½" × 7½"

I *love to collect baskets and scatter them throughout my home, and blue is my favorite color, so it just made sense to combine my two loves in this traditional quilt. A stack of precut 10" squares will provide plenty of fabric for the basket and background pieces, or dig into your scrap basket for larger pieces of your favorite blues and creams.*

Materials

Yardage is based on 42"-wide fabric.

8½" × 8½" square *each* of 16 assorted blue prints for blocks

10½" × 10½" square *each* of 16 assorted light prints for blocks

1¼ yards of blue print for sashing, border, and single-fold binding

2¾ yards of fabric for backing

48" × 48" square of batting

Cutting

Measurements are for machine piecing and include ¼"-wide seam allowances. If you prefer to hand piece the blocks, refer to "For Hand Piecers" on page 33 and do not cut the pieces in this list that are marked with an asterisk.

From *each* blue print square, cut:

1 square, 5⅜" × 5⅜"*

4 squares, 2⅜" × 2⅜"*

From *each* light print square, cut:

1 square, 5⅜" × 5⅜"*

4 squares, 2⅜" × 2⅜"*

2 rectangles, 2" × 5"*

2 squares, 2" × 2"*

From the blue print yardage, cut:

5 strips, 4" × 42"

6 strips, 2" × 42"; crosscut into:

> ⟩ 3 strips, 2" × 35"

> ⟩ 12 rectangles, 2" × 8"

Enough 1¼"-wide *bias* strips to equal 178" when pieced together end to end OR 5 straight-grain strips, 1¼" × 42"

Designed, pieced, and hand quilted by Cindy Blackberg

Making the Blocks

Sew all pieces with right sides together, using a ¼" seam allowance. Press the seam allowances as indicated by the arrows.

1. Select the pieces cut from one blue print and one light print.

2. Draw a diagonal line from corner to corner on the wrong side of each light 5⅜" and 2⅜" square. Layer a marked 5⅜" square on a blue 5⅜" square, right sides together. Sew ¼" from both sides of the drawn line. Cut the unit apart on the marked line to make two half-square-triangle units. Press. The units should measure 5" square, including seam allowances. One unit is extra. Repeat with the dark and light small triangles to make eight small half-square-triangle units measuring 2" square, including seam allowances.

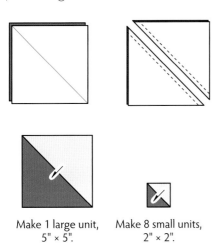

Make 1 large unit, 5" × 5".   Make 8 small units, 2" × 2".

3. Sew three small half-square-triangle units together as shown to make units A and B. Press. The units should measure 2" × 5", including seam allowances.

Make 1 unit A, 2" × 5".   Make 1 unit B, 2" × 5".

4. Sew the A unit to the left edge of the large half-square-triangle unit. Press. Join a light 2" square to the left edge of the B unit; press, and then sew the pieced strip to the top of the unit. Press.

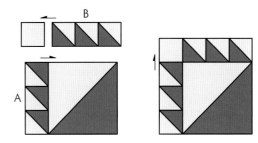

5. Join a small half-square-triangle unit to the end of a light 2" × 5" rectangle. Make two and press. Sew one of these units to the right edge of the unit from step 4; press. Sew the remaining unit to a light 2" square, press, and then sew this unit to the bottom of the unit from step 4 to complete the Basket block. Press. The block should measure 8" × 8", including seam allowances.

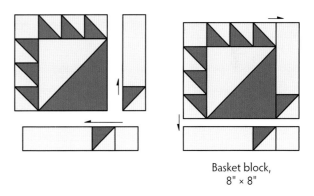

Basket block, 8" × 8"

6. Repeat steps 1–5 to make a total of 16 blocks.

match as you go. Sew the rows and strips together. The quilt top should measure 35" square, including seam allowances.

Quilt assembly

3. Join the blue 4" × 42" strips together end to end to make one long strip. From the pieced strip, cut four strips, 4" × 45". Refer to "Making Borders with Mitered Corners" on page 18 to sew the strips to the quilt top and miter the corners. Press the seam allowances toward the border.

Assembling the Quilt Top

1. Sew together four blocks and three blue 2" × 8" sashing rectangles in alternating positions to make a block row. Press. The row should measure 8" × 35", including seam allowances. Repeat to make a total of four block rows.

Make 4 block rows,
8" × 35".

2. Lay out the block rows and blue 2" × 35" sashing strips in alternating positions. To make sure the blocks align across from one another on opposite sides of the long blue sashing strips, pin

Finishing

For more details on any of the following steps, visit ShopMartingale.com/HowtoQuilt for free downloadable information.

1. Layer the quilt top, batting, and backing. Baste the layers together.

2. Quilt by hand or machine. The quilt shown is hand quilted with an allover Baptist fan design.

3. Use the blue 1¼"-wide strips to make the single-fold binding, and then attach the binding to the quilt. Enjoy!

To make the half-square-triangle units, sew the light and blue triangles together along the long diagonal edges. The diagonal edges are bias, so handle the pieces gently so as not to stretch them.

Refer to "Hand-Piecing Basics" on page 78 to make the templates. Use the templates

to cut the pieces from the fabrics indicated. Cutting instructions are for the Basket blocks only. Patterns do not include seam allowances.

Using the large triangle template, cut:
1 *each* from the light print and blue print for each block (2 total per block)

Using the small triangle template, cut:
8 *each* from the light print and blue print for each block (16 total per block)

Using the rectangle template, cut:
2 from the light print for *each* block

Using the square template, cut:
2 from the light print for *each* block

Optional hand-piecing patterns

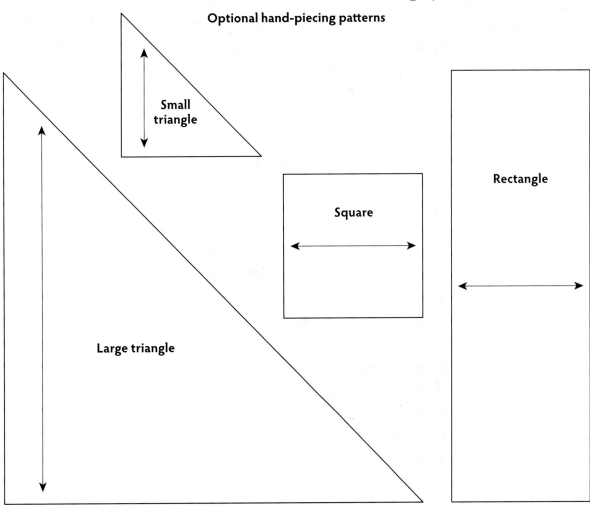

Small triangle

Square

Rectangle

Large triangle

RAILROAD CROSSING

Finished quilt size: 53" × 67"   Finished block size: 8" × 8"

It was love at first sight when a good quilting friend purchased a quilt with this design. Like a mother with children, I know I shouldn't have favorites, but this quilt has been near and dear to my heart ever since I made it. Can you blame me?

Materials

Yardage is based on 42"-wide fabric.

¼ yard *each* of 17 assorted blue prints for blocks and sashing

¼ yard *each* of 16 assorted light prints for blocks and sashing

4" × 8" rectangle *each* of 8 assorted olive prints for blocks

4" × 8" rectangle *each* of 12 assorted cheddar prints for blocks

4" × 8" rectangle *each* of 4 assorted dull gold prints for blocks

4" × 8" rectangle *each* of 12 assorted dark pumpkin prints for blocks

4" × 8" rectangle *each* of 4 assorted light pumpkin prints for blocks

4" × 8" rectangle *each* of 8 assorted dark orange prints for blocks

2 yards of bright blue solid for background

2 yards of dark pumpkin print for inner border

2⅛ yards of black print for outer border and double-fold binding

3⅓ yards of fabric for backing

59" × 73" piece of batting

Paper for foundation piecing

Template plastic

Cutting

Measurements are for machine piecing and include ¼"-wide seam allowances. Trace the A pattern on page 40 onto template plastic and cut it out. Use the template to cut the A pieces from the fabrics indicated. Transfer the reference marks to the seam allowances on the wrong side of each piece. If you prefer to hand piece the quarter circles, refer to "For Hand Piecers" on page 39 and do not cut the pieces in this list that are marked with an asterisk.

From *each of 16* of the assorted blue prints, cut:

2 strips, 2½" × 42"; crosscut into:
  ‣ 15 rectangles, 2" × 2½" (240 total)*
  ‣ 24 rectangles, 1½" × 2½" (384 total)

Continued on page 37

Designed, pieced, and hand quilted by Cindy Blackberg

Continued from page 35

From the remaining blue print, cut:

3 squares, 4⅛" × 4⅛"; cut into quarters diagonally to make 12 side triangles (2 are extra)

6 squares, 2½" × 2½"

2 squares, 2¼" × 2¼"; cut in half diagonally to make 4 corner triangles

From *each* of the assorted light prints, cut:

1 strip, 2½" × 42"; crosscut into 18 rectangles, 2" × 2½" (288 total)*

2 strips, 1½" × 42"; crosscut into 48 squares, 1½" × 1½" (768 total)*

From *each* of the 4" × 8" rectangles, cut:

1 A piece (48 total)

From *12* of the 4" × 8" rectangles, cut:

1 square, 2½" × 2½"

From the bright blue solid, cut:

4 squares, 12½" × 12½"; cut into quarters diagonally to make 16 triangles (2 are extra)

17 squares, 8½" × 8½"

From the *lengthwise grain* of the dark pumpkin print yardage, cut:

2 strips, 1½" × 62"

2 strips, 1½" × 48"

From the *lengthwise grain* of the black print, cut:

2 strips, 4½" × 70"

2 strips, 4½" × 56"

From the remainder of the black print, cut:

Enough 2¼"-wide bias *or* straight-grain strips to equal 250" when pieced together end to end

Making the Blocks

Sew all pieces with right sides together, using a ¼" seam allowance. Press the seam allowances as indicated by the arrows.

1. Trace the arc pattern on page 40 onto paper for foundation piecing 48 times. Using five matching blue 2" × 2½" rectangles and six matching light 2" × 2½" rectangles, paper piece each arc, following the pattern shading for placement of blue and light fabrics. Trim each pieced arc on the outer dashed lines. Carefully remove the foundation paper from each arc.

2. Lay a pieced arc on top of an A piece, right sides together. Line up the point of the light triangles on the arc with the reference marks on the A piece; pin at the reference marks and the ends of the stitching line. Carefully sew along the curved edge, easing in the fullness and taking care not to stretch the pieces as you sew. Press. Repeat to make a total of 48 quarter circles. Press under the seam allowance along the outer curved edge of each piece.

 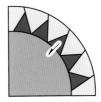

Make 48 quarter circles.

3. Draw a line from corner to corner on the wrong side of each light 1½" square. Place a marked square on one end of a blue print 1½" × 2½" rectangle. Sew on the marked line. Trim ¼" from the stitching line. Press. Repeat on the opposite end of the rectangle with a matching square to make a flying-geese unit. Press. Repeat to make a total of 384 units measuring 1½" × 2½", including seam allowances.

Make 384 units, 1½" × 2½".

4. Sew eight flying-geese units together along their long edges to make a sashing unit. Repeat to make a total of 48 sashing units measuring 2½" × 8½", including seam allowances.

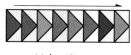

Make 48 units,
2½" × 8½".

Assembling the Quilt Top

1. Referring to the quilt assembly diagram below and working on a design wall or other flat surface, lay out the bright blue solid squares and triangles, the pieced sashing units, the blue print 2½" squares, and the blue print side and corner triangles in diagonal rows. Place the pieced quarter circles on each bright blue square and triangle as shown. When you're pleased with the arrangement, use your favorite method to appliqué the curved edge *only* of each quarter circle in place. Replace each piece on the design wall after you finish it.

2. Sew the pieces in each row together. Press. Join the rows. Press. Add the corner triangles last. Press. The quilt top should measure 43" × 57", including seam allowances.

3. Refer to "Making Borders with Mitered Corners" on page 18 to sew the long dark pumpkin strips to the long black strips and the short dark pumpkin strips to the short black strips along the long edges. Sew the pieced long border strips to the sides of the quilt top and the pieced short border strips to the top and bottom of the quilt top, and miter the corners. Press the seam allowances toward the border.

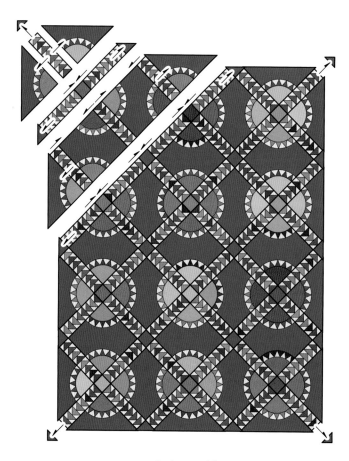

Quilt assembly

Finishing

For more details on any of the following steps, visit ShopMartingale.com/HowtoQuilt for free downloadable information.

1. Layer the quilt top, batting, and backing. Baste the layers together.

2. Quilt by hand or machine. The quilt shown is hand quilted with a fan design in each quarter circle and outline quilting around the arc points and flying-geese units. The background is quilted with a crosshatch design and the borders are quilted with a piano key design.

3. Use the black 2¼"-wide strips to make the double-fold binding, and then attach the binding to the quilt. Enjoy!

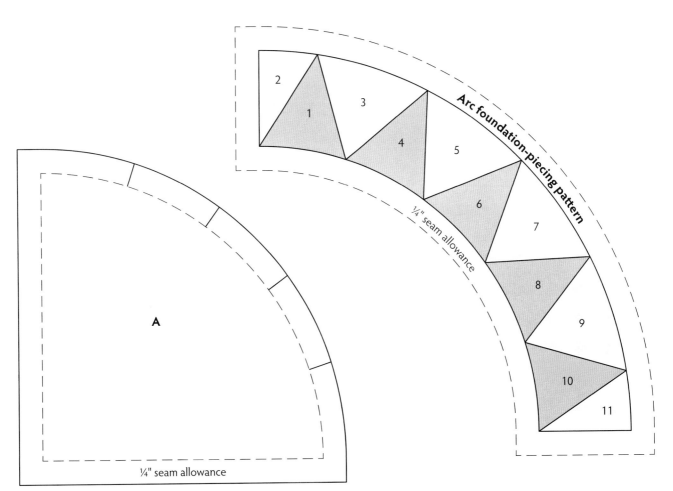

Some quilters like to foundation piece the arcs on a quilt pattern like this, but my preference is for cutting the pieces traditionally using templates and then hand-piecing them together. (I've provided patterns for both methods.)

Lay out your blue and light triangles in the order in which they're pieced together, and then sequentially sew them together. Press the unit. Once you've attached the arc to the quarter circle, trim the light triangles on the ends of the arc with the straight sides of the triangle.

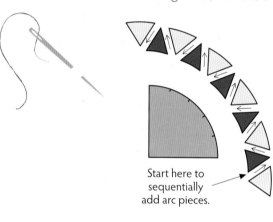

Start here to sequentially add arc pieces.

. . . .

Refer to "Hand-Piecing Basics" on page 78 to make the templates. Use the templates to cut the pieces from the fabrics indicated. Cutting instructions are for the quarter circles only. Patterns do not include seam allowances.

Using template A (quarter circle for hand piecing), cut:

48 from assorted 4" x 8" rectangles

Using template B, cut:

48 sets of 6 matching pieces from the light prints (288 total)

Using template C, cut:

48 sets of 5 matching pieces from the blue prints (240 total)

Optional hand-piecing patterns

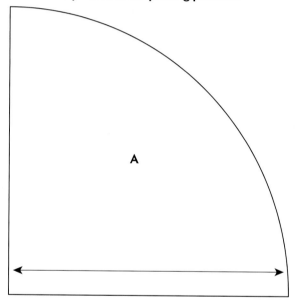

A

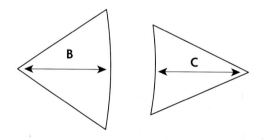

B

C

STAMP BASKET

Finished quilt size: 30½" × 30½"   Finished block size: 6" × 6"

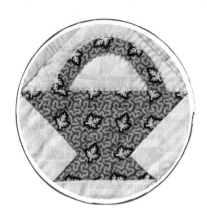

Combine piecing with a wee bit of appliqué to make these adorable Stamp Basket blocks. A traditional favorite, Basket blocks of all kinds are found in antique quilts. These little blocks with appliquéd handles are just the right size for a wall hanging, but I've also made several versions for baby gifts.

Materials

Yardage is based on 42"-wide fabric.

44 squares, 6" × 6", of assorted dark prints for blocks

⅛ yard *each* of 11 assorted light prints for blocks

1 yard of beige check for sashing and border

¼ yard of blue check for single-fold binding

1 yard of fabric for backing

35" × 35" square of batting

Cutting

Measurements are for machine piecing and include ¼"-wide seam allowances. If you prefer to hand piece the blocks, refer to "For Hand Piecers" on page 46 and do not cut the pieces in this list that are marked with an asterisk.

From *each* dark square, cut:

1 bias strip, ¾" × 4½"

1 square, 3⅛" × 3⅛"; cut in half diagonally to make 2 large triangles (1 is extra)*

1 square, 1⅝" × 1⅝"; cut in half diagonally to make 2 small triangles*

From *each* light print, cut:

2 squares, 3⅛" × 3⅛"; cut in half diagonally to make 4 large triangles*

2 squares, 2⅜" × 2⅜"; cut in half diagonally to make 4 medium triangles*

8 rectangles, 1¼" × 2"*

From the beige check, cut:

12 strips, 3½" × 6½"

4 strips, 3½" × 24½"

From the blue check, cut:

Enough 1¼"-wide *bias* strips to total 132" OR 4 straight-grain strips, 1¼" × 42"

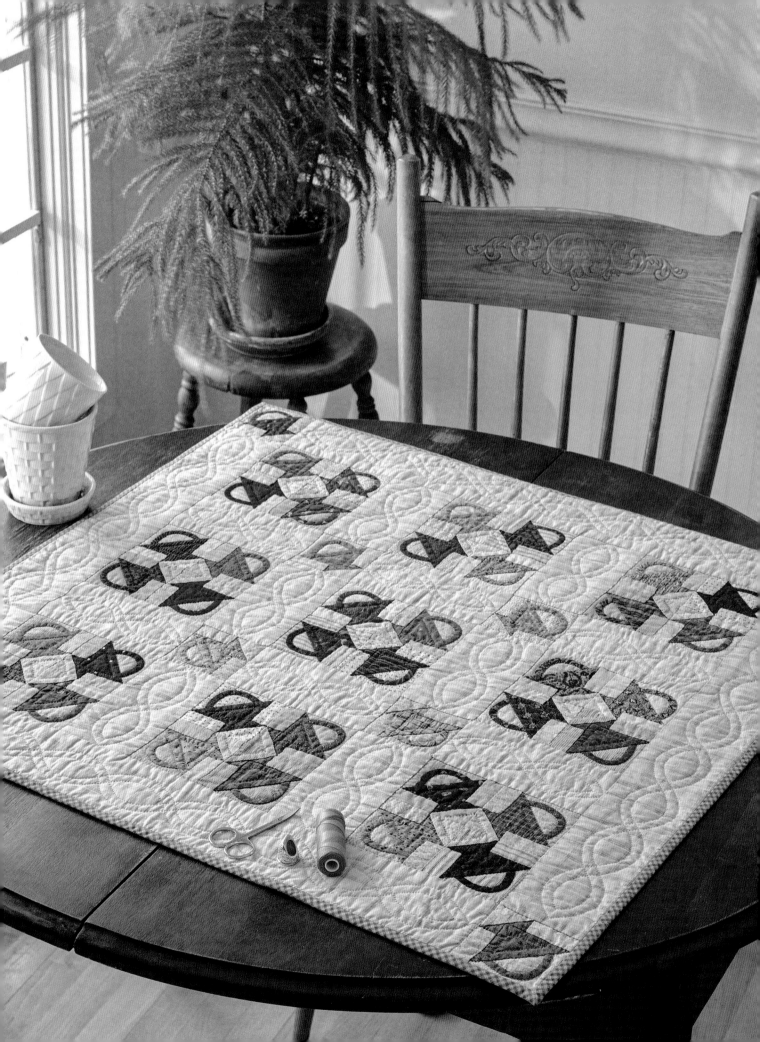

Making the Blocks

Sew all pieces with right sides together, using a ¼" seam allowance. Press the seam allowances as indicated by the arrows.

1. Select the pieces cut from one dark print. From one light print, select one large triangle, one medium triangle, and two rectangles. Press under ¼" on each side of the dark bias strip to make the basket handle.

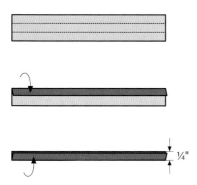

2. Pin the prepared bias strip to the light large triangle, curving it to create the basket handle. Using matching thread, appliqué the handle in place, stitching the inner edge of the strip first. With right sides together, sew the handle triangle to the dark large triangle along the long diagonal edges. Press. The handle unit should measure 2¾" square, including seam allowances.

Make 1 handle unit,
2¾" × 2¾".

3. Stitch a dark small triangle onto the end of each light rectangle as shown. Press.

Make 1 of each unit.

4. Sew the units from step 3 to the sides of the handle unit. Press. Join the light medium triangle to the diagonal edge of the unit. Press. The basket unit should measure 3½" square, including seam allowances.

Make 1 basket unit,
3½" × 3½".

5. Repeat steps 1–4 to make a total of 44 basket units.

6. Arrange four basket units into two rows of two units each. Sew the units in each row together. Join the rows to complete the block. The block should measure 6½" square, including seam allowances. Repeat to make a total of nine blocks. Set aside the remaining eight basket units for the sashing and border.

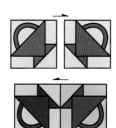 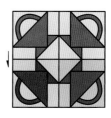

Make 9 blocks,
6½" × 6½".

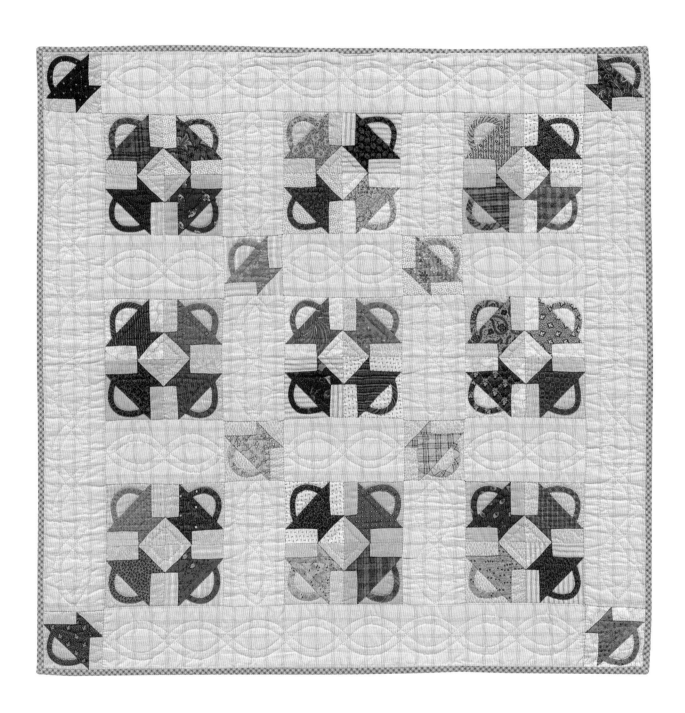

Designed, pieced, appliquéd, and hand quilted by Cindy Blackberg

Assembling the Quilt Top

1. Refer to the quilt assembly diagram below to lay out the blocks, four basket units, and the beige check 3½" × 6½" sashing strips in five horizontal rows. Sew the pieces in each row together. Press. Join the rows. Press. The quilt top should measure 24" square, including seam allowances.

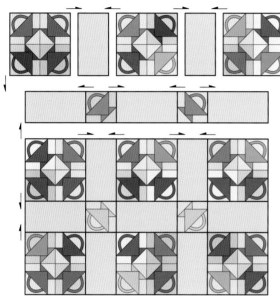

Quilt assembly

2. Refer to the border diagram below to sew beige check 3½" × 24½" strips to the top and bottom of the quilt top. Press. Join basket units to both ends of the remaining two beige check strips, and then sew the pieced strips to the sides of the quilt top. Press.

Finishing

For more details on any of the following steps, visit ShopMartingale.com/HowtoQuilt for free downloadable information.

1. Layer the quilt top, batting, and backing. Baste the layers together.

2. Quilt by hand or machine. The quilt shown is hand quilted. The large triangle of the basket and the square created in the center of each block are outline quilted. The basket handle and the top of the basket are stitched in the ditch. A cable design is quilted in the sashing and border.

3. Use the blue check 1¼"-wide strips to make the single-fold binding, and then attach the binding to the quilt. Enjoy!

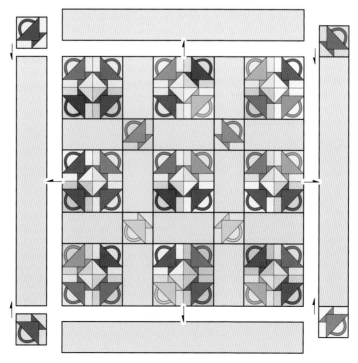

Adding the border

One of the best things about hand piecing is that you can take your project with you. These little blocks make especially great travel companions. Pack your block pieces in a fun tin or box, add thread, hand-sewing needles, a small pair of scissors, a seam ripper, and your thimble, and you're set to sew no matter where you're going.

. . . .

Refer to "Hand-Piecing Basics" on page 78 to make the templates. Use the templates to cut the pieces from the fabrics indicated. Cutting instructions are for the basket units only. Patterns do not include seam allowances.

Using the large triangle template, cut:
1 from *each* dark print (44 total)
4 from *each* light print (44 total)

Using the rectangle template, cut:
8 from *each* light print (88 total)

Using the medium triangle template, cut:
4 from *each* light print (44 total)

Using the small triangle template, cut:
2 from *each* dark print (88 total)

Optional hand-piecing patterns

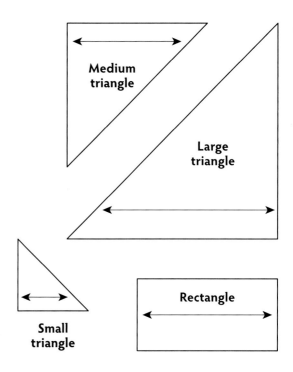

Medium triangle

Large triangle

Small triangle

Rectangle

CHAIN OF STARS

Finished quilt size: 68" × 98"   Finished block size: 15" × 15"

Got the blues? A sure cure is to give your collection of blue prints a home in this celestial two-color quilt. My collection of indigo prints was the perfect choice for me; you may prefer to use just one favorite print or more than the 22 prints called for. There are no wrong choices!

Materials

Yardage is based on 42"-wide fabric.

22 fat eighths of assorted indigo prints for blocks

7¾ yards of light print for background and double-fold binding

6 yards of fabric for backing

76" × 106" piece of batting

Cutting

Measurements are for machine piecing and include ¼"-wide seam allowances. If you prefer to hand piece the blocks, refer to "For Hand Piecers" on page 53 and do not cut the pieces in this list that are marked with an asterisk.

From *each* indigo print, cut:

3 squares, 3" × 3" (66 total)*

24 squares, 1¾" × 1¾" (528 total)*

6 squares, 2⅛" × 2⅛" (132 total; 2 will be extra)

From the light print, cut:

7 strips, 15½" × 42"; crosscut into:

> ⟩ 7 squares, 15½" × 15½"

> ⟩ 10 rectangles, 10½" × 15½"

9 strips, 5½" × 42"; crosscut into 58 squares, 5½" × 5½"

8 strips, 2⅛" × 42"; crosscut into 130 squares, 2⅛" × 2⅛"

33 strips, 1¾" × 42"; crosscut into:

> ⟩ 264 rectangles, 1¾" × 3"*

> ⟩ 264 squares, 1¾" × 1¾"*

Enough 2¼"-wide *bias* strips to equal 344" when pieced together end to end *OR* 9 straight-grain strips, 2¼" × 42"

Making the Blocks

Sew all pieces right sides together, using a ¼" seam allowance. Press the seam allowances as indicated by the arrows.

1. Select the 3" and 1¾" squares cut from one indigo square, 12 light 1¾" × 3" rectangles, and 12 light 1¾" squares. Draw a diagonal line from corner to corner on the wrong side of each indigo 1¾" square.

2. With right sides together, align a marked indigo square on one end of a light rectangle. Sew on the marked line. Trim ¼" from the stitching line. Press. Repeat on the opposite end of the rectangle to make a flying-geese unit. Repeat to make a total of 12 flying-geese units measuring 1¾" × 3", including seam allowances.

Make 12 units,
1¾" × 3".

3. Lay out four flying-geese units with a blue 3" square and four light 1¾" squares in three horizontal rows. Sew the pieces in each row together. Press. Join the rows to make a star unit. Press. Repeat to make a total of three star units. Each unit should measure 5½" × 5½", including seam allowances.

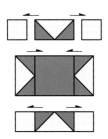 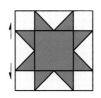

Make 3 star units,
5½" × 5½".

4. Repeat steps 1–3 to make 66 star units total.

5. Lay out five star units and four light 5½" squares in three horizontal rows, alternating positions. Sew the pieces in each row together. Press. Join the rows to make a block. Repeat to make a total of eight blocks. Each block should measure 15½" square, including seam allowances.

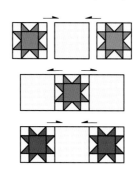 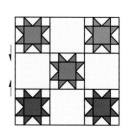

Make 8 blocks,
15½" × 15½".

Making the Side and Corner Units

1. Lay out three star units and three light 5½" squares in two horizontal rows, alternating positions. Sew the pieces in each row together. Press. Join the rows to make a side unit. Repeat to make a total of six units. Each unit should measure 10½" × 15½", including seam allowances.

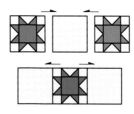 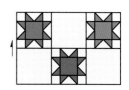

Make 6 side units,
10½" × 15½".

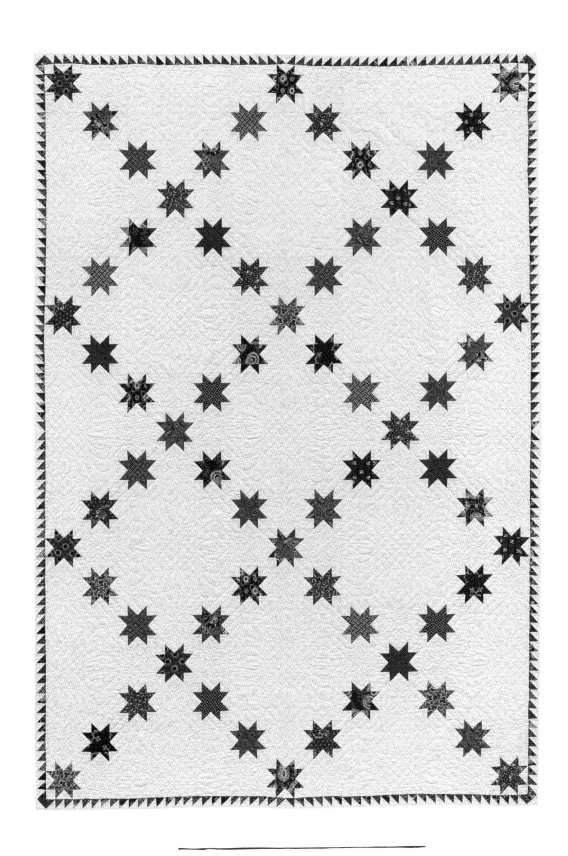

Designed, pieced, and hand quilted by Cindy Blackberg

2. Lay out two star units and two light 5½" squares in two horizontal rows, alternating positions. Sew the pieces in each row together. Press. Join the rows to make a corner unit. Repeat to make a total of four units. Each unit should measure 10½" square, including seam allowances.

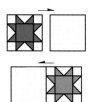

Make 4 corner units,
10½" × 10½".

Assembling the Quilt Top

1. Refer to the quilt assembly diagram at right to lay out the blocks, side units, corner units, light 15½" squares, and light 10½" × 15½" rectangles in seven horizontal rows. Join the pieces in each row. Press. Join the rows. Press. The quilt top should measure 65½" × 95½", including seam allowances.

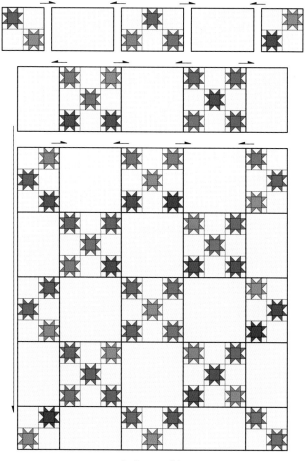

Quilt assembly

2. Draw a diagonal line from corner to corner on the wrong side of each light 2⅛" square. Lay a marked light square on top of an indigo 2⅛" square, right sides together. Sew ¼" from each side of the drawn line. Cut the squares apart on the drawn line to make two half-square-triangle units. Press. The units should measure 1¾" square, including seam allowances. Repeat to make a total of 260 units.

Make 260 units,
1¾" × 1¾".

3. Sew 76 half-square-triangle units in a row, with the 38 units on the left pointing to the right and the 38 units on the right pointing to the left. Press. Repeat to make a total of two side borders measuring 1¾" × 95½", including seam allowances. In the same manner, join 52 triangle units in a row, with the 26 units on the left pointing to the right and the 26 units on the right pointing to the left. Press. Add a triangle unit to each end of the row as shown. Press. Repeat to make a total of two top/bottom borders measuring 1¾" × 68", including seam allowances.

Make 2 side borders,
1¾" × 95½".

Make 2 top/bottom borders,
1¾" × 68".

4. Refer to the border diagram above right to sew the side borders to the sides of the quilt

top. Press. Sew the top and bottom borders to the top and bottom of the quilt top. Press.

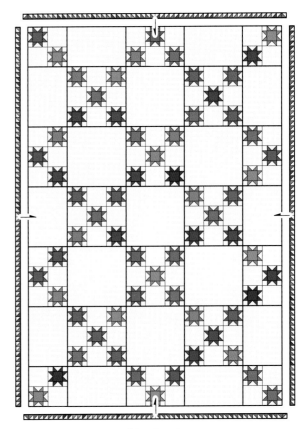

Adding borders

Finishing

For more details on any of the following steps, visit ShopMartingale.com/HowtoQuilt for free downloadable information.

1. Layer the quilt top, batting, and backing. Baste the layers together.

2. Quilt by hand or machine. The quilt shown is hand quilted with a squared feather wreath design in the background squares and units. The border is outline quilted.

3. Use the light 2¼"-wide strips to make the double-fold binding, and then attach the binding to the quilt. Enjoy!

When making the flying-geese units, you'll be joining triangles rather than overlapping and then trimming squares as instructed in steps 1 and 2 of "Making the Blocks." You'll have three points that come together along one side of the unit. To avoid a gap where the points meet, place a smaller triangle on the right edge of the larger triangle, with the straight bottom edges and diagonal edges aligned. The smaller triangle will extend beyond the larger triangle at the top point.

Stitch from the bottom toward the tip of the large triangle, bringing the needle out exactly at the point where the seam allowances cross. Take a small backstitch but do not break the thread. Open out the two pieces, and then place the remaining triangle on the left edge of the larger triangle. Bring the needle through the end of the last stitch, sew to the end of the drawn line, and backstitch.

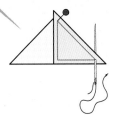 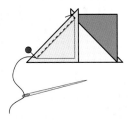

. . . .

Refer to "Hand-Piecing Basics" on page 78 to make the templates. Use the templates to cut the pieces from the fabrics indicated. Cutting instructions are for the star units only. Patterns do not include seam allowances.

Using the large square template, cut:
3 from *each* indigo print (66 total)

Using the small triangle template, cut:
24 from *each* indigo print (528 total)

Using the small square template, cut:
264 from the light print

Using the large triangle template, cut:
264 from the light print

Optional hand-piecing patterns

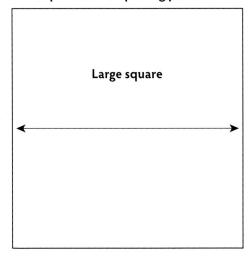

Large square

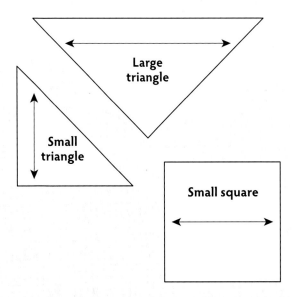

Large triangle

Small triangle

Small square

SUGARLOAF

Finished quilt size: 46" × 47¼"

Up until the late nineteenth century, sugar was sold in the shape of a cone, or sugarloaf, which is how many think this pattern got its name. Even if that isn't the case, this is a sweet quilt to make and it's a great way to put some of your scraps to use.

Materials

Yardage is based on 42"-wide fabric.

8" × 9" scraps of 30 assorted light prints for pieced triangles

6" × 9" scraps of 30 assorted dark prints for pieced triangles

2 yards of dark red print for setting triangles, border triangles, and single-fold binding

1 yard of medium tan print for border triangles

3 yards of fabric for backing

52" × 54" piece of batting

Template plastic

Cutting

Measurements are for machine piecing and include ¼"-wide seam allowances. Before you begin cutting, trace triangle patterns A–C on pages 60 and 61 onto template plastic and cut them out. Use the templates to cut the triangles from the fabrics indicated. If you prefer to hand piece the triangles, refer to "For Hand Piecers" on page 59 and do not cut the pieces in this list that are marked with an asterisk.

From the *lengthwise grain* of *each* assorted light print, cut:
4 strips, 1¾" × 9" (120 total)*

From the *lengthwise grain* of *each* assorted dark print, cut:
3 strips, 1¾" × 9" (90 total)*

From the dark red print, cut:
36 A triangles

12 B triangles

10 C triangles

Enough 1¼"-wide bias strips to equal 200" when pieced together end to end *OR* 5 straight-grain strips, 1¼" × 42"

From the medium tan print, cut:
14 B triangles

12 C triangles

4 rectangles, 2⅜" × 2½"

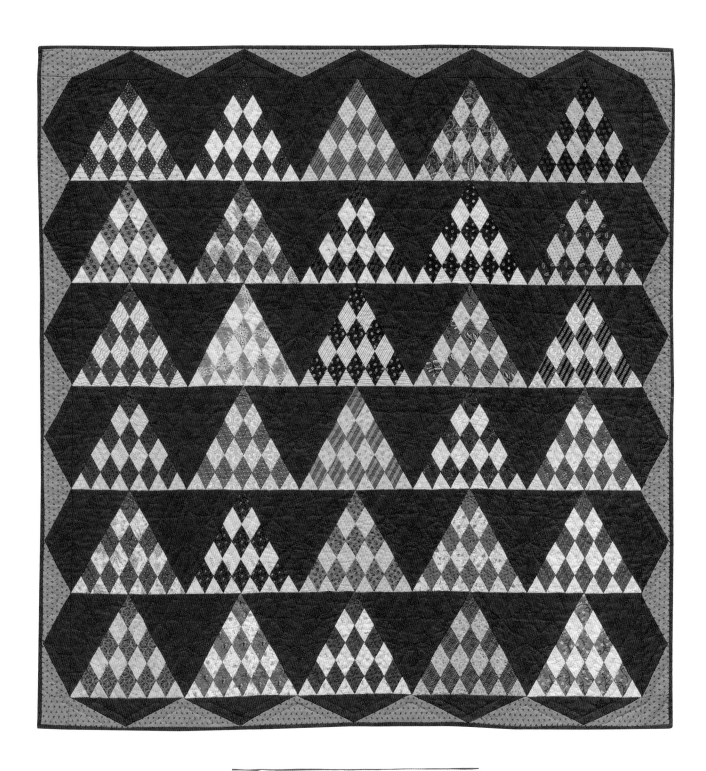

Designed, pieced, and hand quilted by Cindy Blackberg

Making the Pieced Triangles

Sew all pieces with right sides together, using a ¼" seam allowance. Press the seam allowances as indicated by the arrows.

1. Align the 60° line of an acrylic ruler with the bottom of a light print 1¾" × 9" strip and trim the left end of the strip as shown. Measuring 1¾" from the angled cut, make another cut to release the diamond. Continue in this manner to cut a total of 12 diamonds from each light print. Repeat with the dark 1¾" × 9" strips to cut a total of nine diamonds from each print.

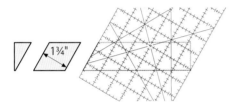

2. Using the diamonds cut from one light print and one dark print, lay out the diamonds in six diagonal rows, alternating the colors as shown. Sew the diamonds in each row together. Press. Join the rows. Press. Repeat to make a total of 30 pieced triangles.

3. Trim the bottom row of light triangles on each pieced triangle ¼" from the points of the dark triangles.

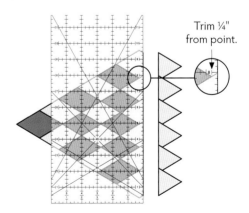

Trim ¼" from point.

Assembling the Quilt Top

1. Refer to the quilt assembly diagram below to lay out the pieced triangles and red A triangles in six horizontal rows of six A triangles and five pieced triangles each, alternating positions. Sew together the triangles in each row. Press. Join the rows. Press.

2. Trim the sides of the quilt top ¼" from the lower point of the pieced triangles.

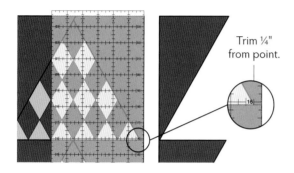

Trim ¼" from point.

3. Sew together seven tan and six red B triangles, alternating positions. Press. Trim the ends of the strip ¼" from the points of the red triangles. The strip should measure 2⅜" × 43¼", including seam allowances. Repeat to make a total of two side borders. Sew the borders to the sides of the quilt top. Press the seam allowances toward the border.

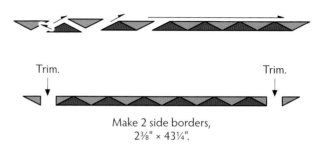

Trim.   Trim.

Make 2 side borders,
2⅜" × 43¼".

Quilt assembly

4. Sew together six tan and five red C triangles, alternating positions. Press. Trim the ends of the strip ¼" from the points of the red triangles. Add a tan 2⅜" × 2½" rectangle to each end of the strip. Press. The strip should measure 2½" × 45¾", including seam allowances. Repeat to make a total of two top/bottom borders. Sew the borders to the top and bottom of the quilt top. Press the seam allowances toward the border.

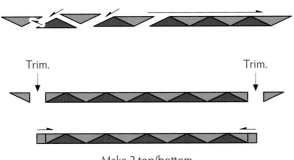

Trim.   Trim.

Make 2 top/bottom
borders, 2½" × 45¾".

Finishing

For more details on any of the following steps, visit ShopMartingale.com/HowtoQuilt for free downloadable information.

1. Layer the quilt top, batting, and backing. Baste the layers together.

2. Quilt by hand or machine. The quilt shown is hand quilted with a five-pointed star in each red triangle. Each pieced triangle is quilted with a chevron design that extends into the red triangles. The border is outline quilted around the inside and outside of the red triangles.

3. Use the red 1¼"-wide strips to make the single-fold binding, and then attach the binding to the quilt. Enjoy!

FOR HAND PIECERS

When hand piecing, there's no need to mark dots or figure out how much you need to stagger the pieces to make the pieces align. Just line up the pencil lines. Your diamond will always line up!

. . . .

Refer to "Hand-Piecing Basics" on page 78 to make the template. Use the template to cut the pieces from the fabrics indicated. Cutting instructions are for the pieced triangles only. The pattern does not include seam allowances.

Optional hand-piecing pattern

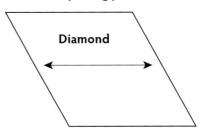

Diamond

Using the diamond template, cut:
12 from *each* light print (360 total)
9 from *each* dark print (270 total)

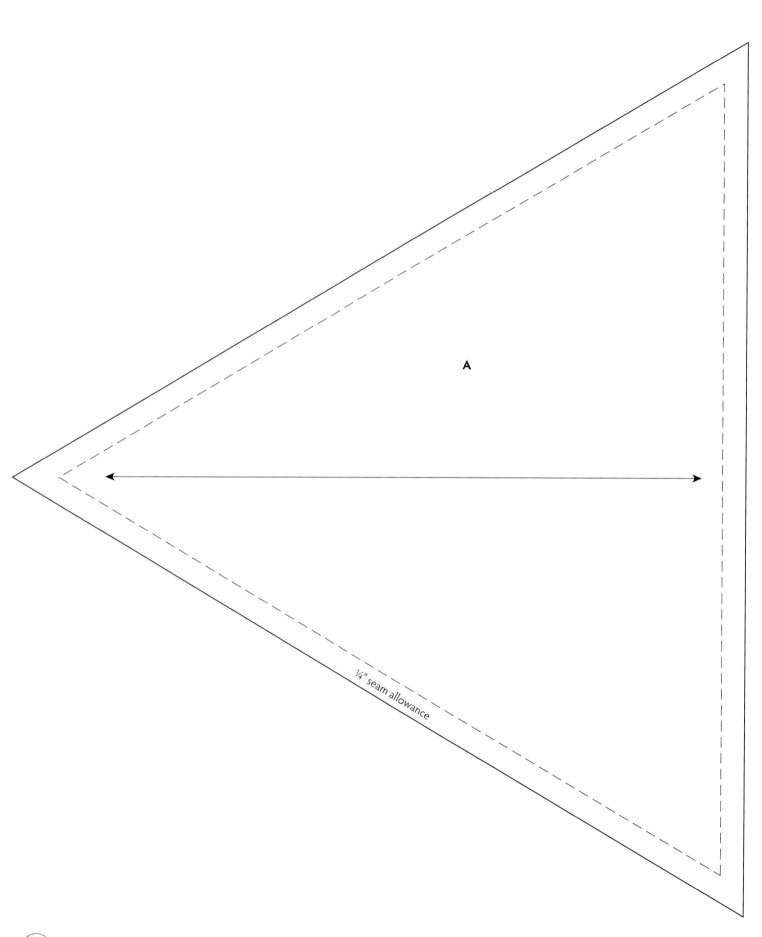

A

¼" seam allowance

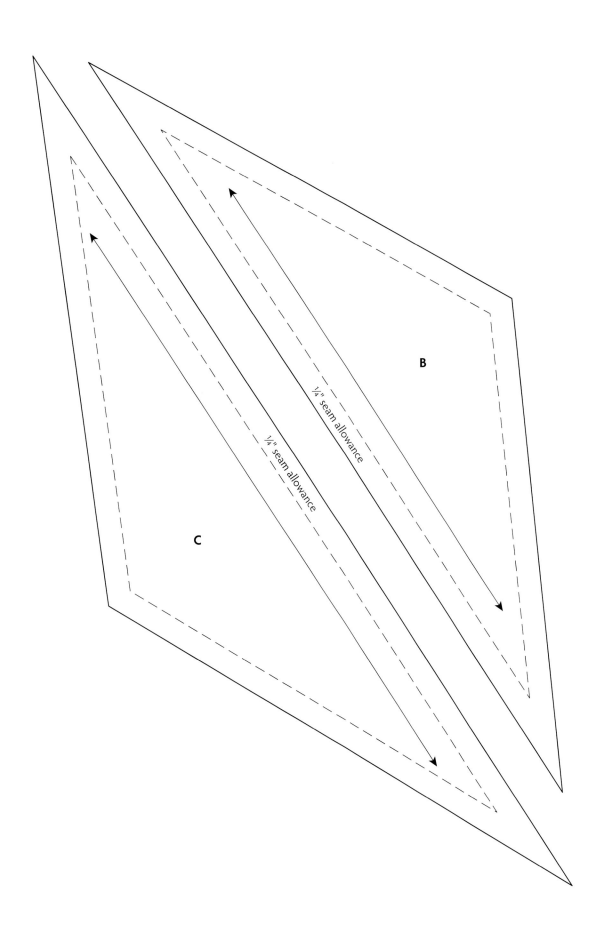

B

¼" seam allowance

¼" seam allowance

C

BLUE BOW TIES

Finished quilt size: 74" × 79⅝"   Finished block size: 4" × 4"

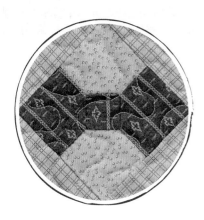

What's a girl to do when she spies a delicious bundle of blue and gray fat quarters? She buys them, of course! I knew immediately that the assortment I used for this quilt was perfect for a bow tie design. This particular version of the Bow Tie block has a square in the middle, which I prefer because it makes a realistic knot. It creates a little more sewing, but the result is spectacular, and I'm sure the special person who receives this would agree!

Materials

Yardage is based on 42"-wide fabric. Fat quarters are 18" × 21".

13 fat quarters of assorted blue and gray prints for blocks (collectively referred to as "blue")

13 fat quarters of assorted light prints for blocks

2⅞ yards of tan check for setting squares

1 yard of black-and-cream stripe for setting triangles

¾ yard of gray-and-tan stripe for binding

5 yards of fabric for backing

80" × 86" piece of batting

Template plastic

Cutting

Measurements are for machine piecing and include ¼"-wide seam allowances. If you prefer to hand piece the blocks, refer to "For Hand Piecers" on page 67 and do not cut the pieces in this list that are marked with an asterisk.

From *each* blue print, cut:

28 squares, 2½" × 2½" (364 total)*

14 squares, 1⅝" × 1⅝" (182 total)*

From *each* light print, cut:

28 squares, 2½" × 2½" (364 total)*

From the tan check, cut:

20 strips, 4½" × 42"; crosscut into 156 squares, 4½" × 4½"

From the *lengthwise grain* of the black-and-cream stripe, cut:

8 strips, 3½" × 36"

From the gray-and-tan stripe, cut:

Enough 2¼"-wide *bias* strips to equal 320" when pieced together end to end OR 8 straight-grain strips, 2¼" × 42"

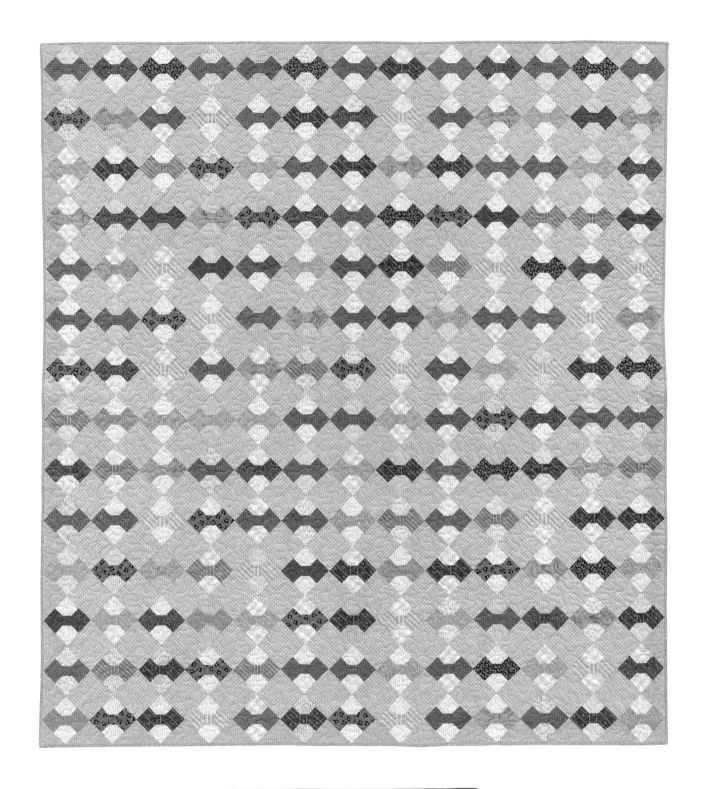

Designed and pieced by Cindy Blackberg; machine quilted by Cathy Witt

Additional Cutting

1. Trace the bow tie cutting guide on page 66 onto template plastic and cut it out. Tape the guide to the right side of a rotary ruler that's at least as large as the guide, aligning the short edge with the edge of the ruler. Place the ruler over a 2½" blue square so the guide covers all but one corner. Cut off the corner extending beyond the ruler. Repeat with the remaining blue and light 2½" squares.

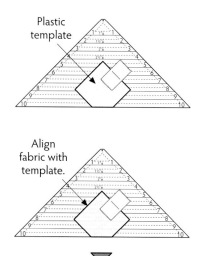

2. To cut the setting triangles, align the 45° line of an acrylic ruler with the bottom of a black-and-cream stripe 3½" × 36" strip and trim the left end of the strip as shown. Rotate the ruler so the 45° line of the ruler is aligned with the top of the strip, and cut the opposing angle of the triangle. Continue rotating the ruler back and forth to cut triangles the length of the strip. Repeat with the remaining strips to cut a total of 54 triangles.

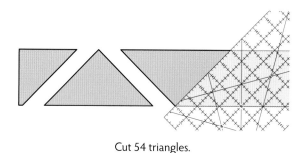

Cut 54 triangles.

Making the Blocks

Sew all pieces with right sides together, using a ¼" seam allowance. Press the seam allowances as indicated by the arrows.

1. Select two matching trimmed blue squares, a matching blue 1⅝" square, and two matching trimmed light squares. Sew trimmed blue squares to opposite sides of the 1⅝" square. Press.

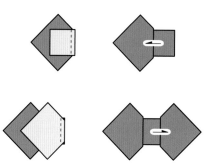

2. Place a trimmed light square over one of the trimmed blue squares, right sides together. Starting at the outer edge, sew the right edges together, stopping ¼" from the corner. With the needle down, pivot the piece and line up the trimmed edge of the light square with the edge of the knot; stitch, stopping ¼" from the corner. Pivot again, and stitch the remaining side of the light square to the bow. Press. Repeat to inset the remaining trimmed light square into the opposite side of the bow. Press. The block should measure 4½" square, including seam allowances.

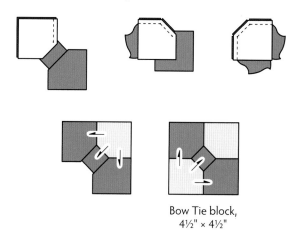

Bow Tie block,
4½" × 4½"

3. Repeat steps 1 and 2 to make a total of 182 blocks.

Assembling the Quilt Top

Refer to the quilt assembly diagram below to lay out the blocks, the tan checked setting squares, and the black stripe setting triangles in diagonal rows. Sew the pieces in each row together. Join the rows. Add the corner triangles last. Trim the corners even with the edges of the quilt top.

Finishing

For more details on any of the following steps, visit ShopMartingale.com/HowtoQuilt for free downloadable information.

1. Layer the quilt top, batting, and backing. Baste the layers together.

2. Quilt by hand or machine. The quilt shown is machine quilted with an allover stippling design.

3. Use the gray-and-tan stripe 2¼"-wide strips to make double-fold binding, and then attach the binding to the quilt. Enjoy!

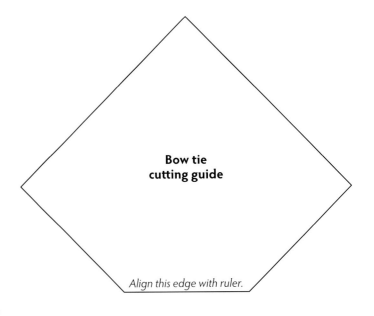

Bow tie cutting guide

Align this edge with ruler.

Quilt assembly

FOR HAND PIECERS

Hand piecing the blocks for this charmer is the same as for machine piecing, although it's much easier in my opinion! You can skip step 1 of "Additional Cutting" because the template is already the required shape. The diagonal edge of each piece is on the bias, so be careful not to stretch the edge as you're sewing. Also be careful not to get too carried away making these blocks, the way I did—I made enough blocks to make the quilt, plus a baby quilt and a few pillows.

Refer to "Hand-Piecing Basics" on page 78 to make the templates. Use the templates to cut the pieces from the fabrics indicated. Cutting instructions are for the Bow Tie blocks only. Patterns do not include seam allowances.

Using the bow tie template, cut:

28 from *each* blue print (364 total)

28 from *each* light print (364 total)

Using the square template, cut:

14 from *each* blue print (182 total)

Optional hand-piecing patterns

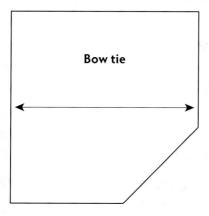

Bow tie

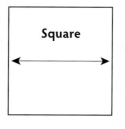

Square

APPLE OF MY EYE

Finished quilt size: 24¾" × 35¾"

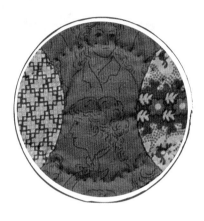

Ready to up your hand-stitching skills? The apple core pattern will do just that, giving you plenty of practice stitching gently curved convex and concave edges. Like Little Houses (page 73), this is a charm quilt, so take advantage of the opportunity to dive into your scrap bag and use some of your smaller pieces. I cut out twice as many shapes and doubled my fun, making one quilt for myself and one for my quilting friend Jo Morton.

Materials

Yardage is based on 42"-wide fabric. Fat quarters are 18" × 21".

187 squares, 4" × 4", of assorted medium and dark prints for apple core pieces

1 fat quarter of navy print for single-fold bias binding

1¼ yards of fabric for backing

30" × 42" piece of batting

Template plastic

Hand-piecing supplies

Cutting

Measurements include ¼" seam allowances. Before you begin cutting, trace the apple core pattern on page 72 onto template plastic and cut it out. Using the template and referring to "Hand-Piecing Basics" on page 78, cut the pieces from the fabrics indicated. Extend the reference marks given on each side of the template ¼" beyond the traced lines so that they extend into the seam allowances when the pieces are cut out.

From *each* of the medium and dark prints, cut:
1 apple core piece (187 total)

From the navy print, cut:
Enough 1¼"-wide *bias* strips to equal 150" when pieced together end to end

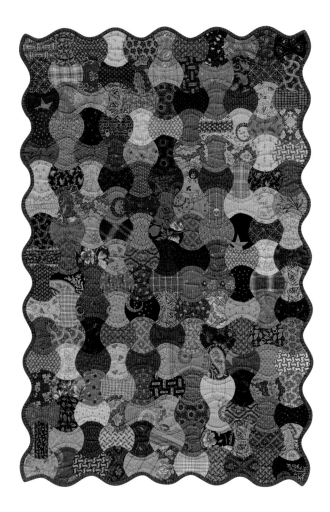

Designed, hand pieced, and
hand quilted by Cindy Blackberg

Assembling the Quilt Top

Refer to "Hand-Piecing Basics" on page 78 and
"Hand Sewing Curved Edges" at right.

1. Using a design wall or another flat surface,
refer to the quilt assembly diagram on page 72 to
lay out the apple core pieces in 17 horizontal rows
of 11 pieces each. Sew the pieces in each row
together.

2. Join the rows. To sew the rows together, lay
one row on top of another row. Sew *only the
concave side* of the shapes as you did when
assembling the rows.

1. Place two apple core pieces right
sides together, matching the concave
(curves out) side on top of the convex
side (curves in) of the other piece. Pin
at the center markings.

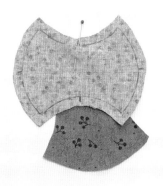

2. When sewing, you'll *always* sew
with the concave side on top. Insert
your needle through both pieces at the
beginning of the marked seamline and
backstitch.

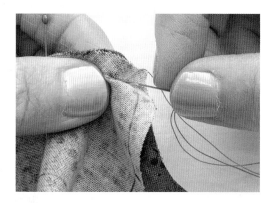

3. Sew along the marked seamline and backstitch when you reach the center pin. Remove the pin and use it to pin the two pieces together at the opposite corner.

4. Continue sewing until you reach the pin at the corner. Remove the pin and take two backstitches. Clip the thread, leaving a ½"-long tail.

5. To join rows, pin and sew two pieces at a time, always with the concave piece on top. That means you'll stitch every other shape across the row, leaving the piece with convex curves unsewn.

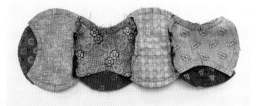

6. After sewing half the shapes together across the row, turn the work over so the unsewn pieces now have the concave curve on top. Sew the remainder of the pieces together to complete the row.

7. When all pieces are joined, the seam allowances will naturally lie toward the convex sides of the shape. There's no need to press until the entire quilt top is finished. Notice how the seam intersections form little four patches when pressing is complete.

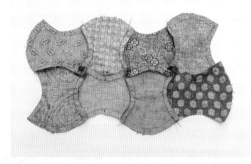

3. Turn the rows around and sew the remaining concave sides. Press the way the seam allowances want to lie. Repeat to sew the remaining rows together.

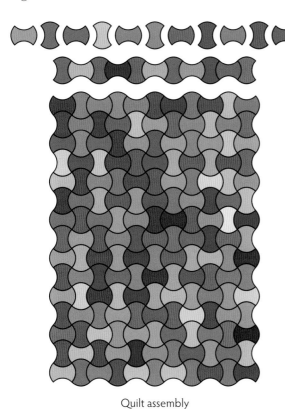

Quilt assembly

Finishing

For more details on any of the following steps, visit ShopMartingale.com/HowtoQuilt for free downloadable information.

1. Layer the quilt top, batting, and backing. Baste the layers together.

2. Quilt by hand or machine. The quilt shown is outline quilted by hand.

3. Use the navy 1¼"-wide bias strips to make the single-fold binding, and then attach the binding to the quilt. I attached the binding by hand as well. Enjoy!

Pattern does not include seam allowances.

Hand-piecing pattern

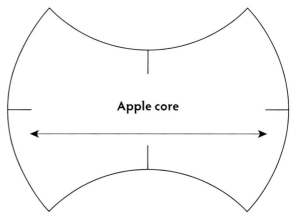

Apple core

LITTLE HOUSES

Finished quilt size: 20½" × 21¾"

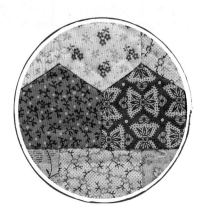

Charming in more ways than one, this sweet little quilt is easy to love. A true charm quilt, where no fabric is repeated, Little Houses is the perfect opportunity for using little scraps of fabric. Because the shapes are much better suited to hand piecing than machine sewing, instructions are given for hand piecing only.

Materials

Yardage is based on 42"-wide fabric.

40 squares, 3" × 3", of assorted dark prints for houses

45 squares, 3" × 3", of assorted light prints for houses

¼ yard of blue print for inner border

⅓ yard of brown print for outer border

¼ yard of brown stripe for single-fold binding

¾ yard of fabric for backing

25" × 26" square of batting

Template plastic

Hand-piecing supplies

Cutting

Measurements include ¼" seam allowances. Before you begin cutting, trace the pattern on page 77 onto template plastic and cut it out. Using your template and referring to "Hand-Piecing Basics" on page 78, cut the pieces from the fabrics indicated.

From *each* of the dark prints, cut:
1 house piece (40 total)

From *each* of the light prints, cut:
1 house piece (45 total)

From the blue print, cut:
4 strips, 1" × 21"

From the brown print, cut:
2 strips, 2" × 24"
2 strips, 2" × 26"

From the brown stripe, cut:
Enough 1¼"-wide *bias* strips to equal 95" when pieced together end to end OR 3 straight-grain strips, 1¼" × 42"

Assembling the Rows

Refer to "Hand-Piecing Basics" on page 78 as needed.

1. Lay two dark house pieces right sides together. Place a pin through the left corner of the top piece and match the left corner of the bottom piece. Hand sew the pieces together, backstitching at the beginning and end to secure the stitches and leaving a thread tail about ½" long at the end.

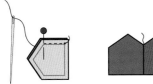

2. Add six more house pieces to make a row. Make a total of five dark rows.

Make 5 dark rows.

3. Repeat steps 1 and 2 with nine light pieces to make a light row. Make a total of five light rows.

Make 5 light rows.

Designed, hand pieced, and hand quilted by Cindy Blackberg

Assembling the Quilt Top

1. Refer to the quilt assembly diagram on page 77 to arrange the rows in alternating positions.

2. To sew the rows together, lay a light row on top of a dark row. Place a pin at the corner of a light house and into the seam allowance of a dark house. Make sure the seam allowance is to the left. Stitch to the pin, pull the seam allowance to the right, and place a pin at the end of the next seam. You'll be sewing up and down all along the

pencil lines, avoiding the seam allowances. Repeat with each pair of light and dark rows to make a total of five double rows.

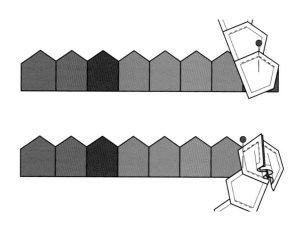

3. Sew the rows together along their long straight edges. Press the seam allowances in either direction.

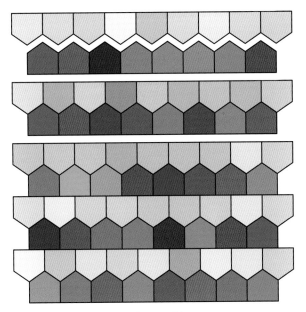

Quilt assembly

4. Trim the light houses along each side in line with the sides of the dark house.

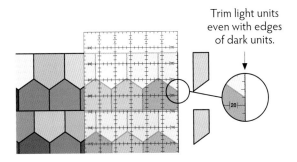

Trim light units even with edges of dark units.

5. Refer to "Making Borders with Mitered Corners" on page 18 to join each blue strip to a brown strip. Sew the long strips to the sides of the quilt top, and sew the short strips to the top and bottom of the quilt top, mitering the corners. Press the seam allowances toward the border.

Finishing

For more details on any of the following steps, visit ShopMartingale.com/HowtoQuilt for free downloadable information.

1. Layer the quilt top, batting, and backing. Baste the layers together.

2. Quilt by hand or machine. The light houses in the quilt shown are outline quilted by hand along the top and bottom of each shape. The blue border and the dark houses are not quilted. The brown border is quilted with a straight line through the center.

3. Use the brown stripe 1¼"-wide strips to make the single-fold binding, and then attach the binding to the quilt. Enjoy!

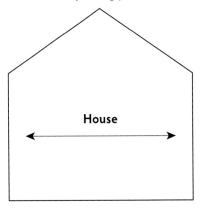

Hand-piecing pattern

House

Pattern does not include seam allowances.

HAND-PIECING BASICS

I am a hand piecer at heart, and it's usually my preferred method for making a quilt. In fact, I hand pieced most of the quilts in this book. But I understand that not everyone is like me, so I've given machine-piecing instructions for making the quilts in this book—except for Apple of My Eye (page 69) and Little Houses (page 73), which are both better suited to hand piecing. The option for hand piecing, however, is included for all the quilts, so if you've never tried piecing by hand or you just need a refresher, the basics are covered in this section. I think you'll find that hand piecing goes quickly once you get into a rhythm, and it can be very calming.

Hand vs. Machine

While it would seem that the only difference between hand piecing and machine piecing is the equipment used to sew the pieces together, there are a couple of other major differences.

› Templates are used to cut out hand-pieced patches, and the templates *do not* include seam allowances. Seam allowance is added to the pieces as you cut them out.

› In hand piecing, you don't stitch over seam allowances, and you don't press the seam allowances until an entire section is completed.

Supplies

One of the joys of hand piecing is that very few supplies are needed, which makes projects very portable—another benefit! You can literally stitch just about anywhere, something you couldn't do if you were machine piecing and needed electricity. Here's the short list of supplies.

› Size 10 or 11 sharp needles

› Hand-quilting thread. I almost exclusively use J&P Coats Dual Duty thread in the color "dogwood." The cotton-covered polyester hand-quilting thread is coated with a sleek finish and glides through the fabric without knotting excessively.

› Thimble. I can't work without a thimble. I use it for piecing, embroidery, appliqué, and quilting, and wear it on the middle finger of my right hand (I'm right-handed).

› Scissors. My favorite scissors for cutting my pieces are Karen Kay Buckley's 7½" serrated-edge scissors. I also keep a smaller pair of scissors handy for snipping threads.

› Pins with a fine shaft

› Template plastic

› Mechanical pencil. I use a pencil with 0.9 mm lead for tracing around the templates

Making the Templates

1. Trace the patterns given with the project onto template plastic, using a mechanical pencil. Be sure to mark the piece name or letter, grain line, and any reference marks.

2. Cut out the pieces exactly on the marked lines. Your fabric pieces will only be as accurate as your templates, so it's always a good idea to lay templates back over the patterns and make sure they're accurate.

Cutting the Fabric Pieces

1. Lay your fabric wrong side up on a rotary-cutting mat or sandpaper board. A sandpaper board will keep your fabric from slipping and aid in more accurate tracing.

2. Place the template on the fabric, leaving enough space around the edges to add seam allowance as you're cutting out the piece. Make sure the grain line marked on the template is aligned with the lengthwise grain line of the fabric. Using the mechanical pencil, trace around the template. Trace any additional shapes required from the same fabric, leaving at least ½" between each shape.

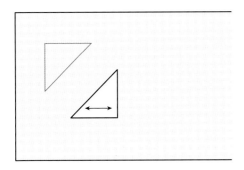

3. Cut out the shapes ¼" beyond the marked line. Just eyeball the measurement. You'll be lining up the marked lines to sew on, so it isn't crucial that every seam allowance is a perfect ¼". The more pieces you cut, the better you'll get at estimating the distance.

Sewing the Pieces

1. Lay out your pieces as they'll be sewn.

2. Pick up the first two pieces to be joined and place them right sides together. With the seam line you'll be sewing positioned at the top, push a pin through the end point of the seam on the top piece, matching up the point of the seam on the bottom piece as you push it through. Leave the pin hanging. (Left-handed piecers should place the pin in the right corner.)

3. Thread your sewing needle with approximately a 12" to 18" length of thread. Make a small knot in one end.

4. Insert the needle at the top right corner on the pencil line and find the bottom corner with your needle. Pull the needle through and take a backstitch. Your knot will be on top.

5. Stitch along the pencil line, using small stitches. End by coming up in the corner at the end of the marked line where the pin is. Remove the pin and backstitch twice. Cut the thread, leaving a ½" tail.

6. Continue sewing pieces together in this manner. When sewing opposing seams, place a pin *before* the seam allowances, going through the front to the back. Sew up to the seam allowances, bringing the needle up exactly at the corner pin; backstitch and tug gently on the thread. Flip up the top seam allowances and go straight through to the other side. Flip the bottom seam allowances to the right. Backstitch and tug on this side of the seam allowances. The seam allowances will be free to press one way or the other.

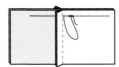 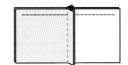

ABOUT THE AUTHOR

Cindy began quilting in 1976, during America's bicentennial. Her first quilts were for her two small sons and other family members. When her quilts caught the eye of a local quilt-shop owner, she began her teaching career. In 1992 Cindy won the International Quilt Festival's Jewel Pearce Patterson award for teaching excellence. From then until her retirement in 2014, Cindy taught handwork, her specialty, across the United States. She continues to make scrappy traditional quilts, mostly by hand, using reproduction fabrics.